COINS OF THE BIBLE

A GUIDE OF BIBLICAL HISTORY AND COINS

TABLE OF CONTENTS

Art Director: Matthew W. Jeffirs • Book Design: Robert A. Cashatt • Editor: Teresa Lyle

All rights reserved. No part of this publication may be reproduced in whole or in part, or stored in a retrieval system or transmitted in any form or by an means, electronic, mechanical, including photocopying, recording or otherwise, without written permission of the publisher.
The coins in this folder are finely detailed replicas of the original coins.
Correspondence concerning this book's contents should be directed to the publisher.

Whitman
Publishing, LLC
PUBLISHING SINCE 1934

3101 Clairmont Road, Suite C
Atlanta, Georgia 30329
Copyright © 2004 Whitman Publishing, LLC, Atlanta, GA
ISBN: 0-7948-1810-2
Printed in China

COINS OF THE BIBLE

Coins provide a unique vista into another culture's values and mores. They generally depict the historical and symbolic figures important to specific societies and illuminate a culture's most cherished beliefs. Whether you are looking at a half shekel, a tribute penny, a widow's mite, or a coin minted today, you can, with some effort, determine the strength and the vision of the country that minted its coinage. You can literally access new worlds through learning about coins!

Studying ancient coinage is certainly a fascinating pursuit, but have you ever wondered what it was like before coins were minted? People relied on bartering as a means of exchange. Let's consider what kinds of items might have been used for trade. A farmer might have lent a hoe or shovel to his neighbor in exchange for items he needed. A neighbor might have exchanged an amphora of oil for barley.

Or a baker might have given someone bread for fruit, olive oil, flour, or some other item. And there were, of course, opportunities for trading services; one person might have agreed to cook in exchange for someone taking care of an infant or helping harvest a field. Whatever the exchange, both parties had to agree on terms fair to both, and bartering was initially and generally a reasonable way to procure goods and services. In fact, even after the introduction of coins, sometime in the seventh century, bartering continued, as it does today. But bartering had its limitations, and those were that common possessions of value such as cattle and foodstuffs were perishable and, moreover, not easily transportable. This led to gold, silver, and bronze being used for coinage; all these malleable metals were durable and convenient to transport. Wealth, to be useful, had to have permanent imperishable properties. These precious metals answered the problem.

When societies began to grow, to make the transition from hunter/gatherer (nomadic) life to early settlements, people from many cultures might settle into an area, indeed as they did in Judea, and this created a cosmopolitan administrative and economic center of commerce, where there arose a need for specific commodities, and so arose the need for coinage and a standard system of valuation. Likewise, when regime change occurred, from Persian, to Grecian, to Roman, this helped fuel the need for coinage. If one country conquered another, it transported not only some of its citizens but also its cultural values and at least remnants of its own system of commerce.

Concurrently, people began to rely on other lands for specific wares, special commodities, luxury items, if you will, that that society might not or could not produce; therefore, merchants became vital to emergent economies. Trade with other regions required such middlemen who could travel and procure goods, then return home and sell them. Of course, this meant that there must be a means of exchanging one currency for another, an agreed upon value among different and competing currencies, so money-changers, in addition to tradesmen, grew in number.

During Biblical days, merchants and moneychangers generally met in the great Temple, a place of enormous religious and cultural significance to the Jewish people.

King Solomon, son of David, built the first Temple: *"Solomon, my son, whom alone God hath chosen, is yet young and tender, and the work is great; for the palace [Temple] is not for man, but for the Lord God"* (First Chronicles 29: 1). Solomon received financial help from his father and materials, mainly cedar wood from Lebanon, and skilled manpower from Hiram, the Phoenician King of Tyre. Even with this assistance, the Hebrews were forced to pay huge taxes for the Temple's construction and this led to turmoil.

The Temple on Mount Moriah began 480 years after the Hebrew exodus from Egypt (1 Kings 6: 1) and it took approximately 70,000 men, working over seven years, to complete the structure. It had an east-to west orientation and was divided into three parts, each leading into another. This vast and magnificent structure caused Jerusalem to be seen as the spiritual and political capital of the Jewish people.

After King Solomon died in 922 B.C., violence erupted and the new king, Solomon's son Rehoboam, refused to lower taxes and stop enforced labor, and many Jewish tribes withdrew to another area of land in the north, which they called Israel, and Rehoboam was left to rule the southern kingdom called Judah.

Unfortunately, Israel was not stable and fell to the Assyrians in 722 B.C. Although Judah withstood the Assyrians, it was later conquered by the Babylonians who came and took the Jews captive and burned the first Temple to the ground in 586 B.C.

Although there were attempts to rebuild the Temple, it was not until Judea was under Roman control and Herod became King of Judea in 40 B.C. that a Temple on scale with the first one would be started. Construction began in 19 B.C. and it took 46 years (John 2: 20) and was not completed until after Herod's death.

The new Temple was significantly larger than the first and was open to Jew as well as gentile. But like its predecessor, the Temple was later destroyed through conflict but its historical significance is still an integral source of spirituality for the Jewish community.

Men and women made yearly pilgrimages to the holy Temple of Jerusalem and there they bought animals for religious sacrifice and paid their "sacred" tributes. But despite this sanctity of the Temple, moneychangers often took advantage of their position and charged exchange rates worthy of usurers. Today, if you travel to most European countries, you must exchange the U.S. dollar for a determined number of Euros, (what's been agreed upon by market demands), and you will likely incur a minimal service charge for the exchange, but nothing by comparison to the profit these moneychangers made.

Competition was no doubt stiff among the "bankers" and dealers and each competed with one another in the outer court of the Temple, each attempting to establish his bench as close to the Temple door as possible.

Such unholy actions and exorbitant usurer rates, often eight percent or more, were practices that incurred the ire of Jesus, and we recall the memorable moment when: *"Jesus went into the temple of God and cast out all them that sold and bought in the temple, and overthrew the tables of the moneychangers and the seats of them that sold doves. / And said unto them, It is written my house shall be called the house of prayer, but ye have made it a den of thieves"* (Matthew 21: 12-13).

Of course, as commerce is necessary to any society, so is taxation for public projects and civil maintenance. Jerusalem was no exception. There were two kinds of tribute money in ancient Judea: the sacred and the civil. The sacred or "atonement" money was the half shekel mandated by Moses; every man 20 years of age

or older was obliged to pay this amount when the Israelites were first numbered. *"This they shall give, every one that passeth among them that are numbered, half a shekel after the shekel of the sanctuary: (a shekel is twenty coin gerahs:) an half shekel shall be the offering of the LORD"* (Exodus 30: 13). Later under Joshua (2 Chronicles 24: 4-14) it was the annual tribute for Temple repairs. After the Babylonian captivity the tax was one-third shekel voluntarily paid *"for the service of the house of our God"* (Nehemiah 10: 32). The tax was a half shekel once more when the Jews were dispersed and was known as the Temple tax for the upkeep of the temple, though the Jewish priest class was not without its own scoundrels and much of the money designated for the Temple was pocketed immorally and illegally.

The second form of tax was a toll for the public use of bridges and gates.

We can recall this form of taxation by Jesus' proclamation: *"Render therefore to all their dues: tribute to whom tribute is due, custom to whom custom; fear to whom fear; honor to whom honor"* (Romans 13: 7). There was also a tax levied by the Roman emperor Caesar Augustus when Judea became a Roman province. This was the tax that took Joseph and Mary to Bethlehem, as these taxes had to be paid in the town of one's birth.

While the average citizen no doubt found the taxation and required sacrifices such as animals, grain, and wine, burdensome, only a few dared publicly denounce them for fear of recompense.

The Romans tried to bate Jesus into just such a position by getting him to profess that only the sacred temple taxes should be paid: *"Is it lawful to pay tribute to Caesar or not? / But Jesus perceived their wickedness, and said, Why tempt ye me, ye hypocrites? / Show me the tribute money"* (Matthew 22: 17-19). They brought one and Jesus asked them whose image and inscription it was. They said Caesar's and Jesus surprised them with perhaps the best known New Testament reference to the tribute penny:

"Render unto Caesar, the things which are Caesar's, and to God the things which are God's" (Matthew 22: 21).

The penny is mentioned in other scriptural passages:

"But the same servant went out, and found one of his fellow servants, which owed him an hundred pence: and he laid hands on him, and took him by the throat saying, Pay me that thou owest" (Matthew 18: 28).

"Why was this waste of the ointment made? For it might have been sold for three hundred pence and given to the poor?" (Mark 14: 4-5; John 12: 5).

"He took out two pence, and gave them to the host, and said unto him, Take care of him; and whatsoever thou spendest more, when I come again, I will repay thee" (Luke 10: 35).

"And I heard a voice in the midst of the four beasts say, A measure of wheat for a penny, and three measures of barley for a

penny; and all thou hunt not the oil and the wine"
(Revelations 6: 6).

The tribute penny, also known as a Roman denarius, was slightly less than a day's wage, no small amount for agricultural laborers and peasants. It was from the reign of Tiberius and the portrait on the coin's obverse is the emperor, with the inscription: "Tiberius, Caesar Augustus, Son of the Divine Augustus." The reverse shows a seated female, generally believed to be Livia, Tiberius' mother, with the inscription "High Priest."

The tribute penny was, of course, not the only coin in circulation in Jerusalem. Many smaller denominations existed.

The lepton, a bronze coin often called a mite, was probably the smallest coin known to the Jews. This coin's obverse depicts an 8 rayed star and the reverse an upside down anchor. Its representation appeared on many coins.

The most famous Biblical reference to the lepton is the story of the widow's mite:

"And Jesus sat over against the treasury, and beheld how the people cast money into the treasury: and many that were rich cast in much. / And there came a certain poor widow and she threw in two mites, which make a farthing. / And he called unto him his disciples, and saith unto them, Verily I say unto you. That this poor widow hath cast more in, than all they which have cast into the treasury: / For all they did cast in of their abundance, but she of her want did cast in all that she had . . ." (Mark 12: 41-44).

The mite is mentioned in other scriptural passages:

"I tell thee, thou, shalt not depart thence, till thou has paid the very last mite" (Luke 12: 59).

But the widow's mite story best illustrates a primary tenant of Christ's teachings: it is better to give from the heart than from a sense of obligation. To put the widow's gift into perspective, it would have taken 200 leptons or widow's mites to make one silver denarius.

THE HALF SHEKEL

OBVERSE

LAUREATE BUST OF MELKART

LION'S SKIN

Laureate bust of Melkart, a pagan deity, facing right with a lion's skin tied around his neck.

REVERSE

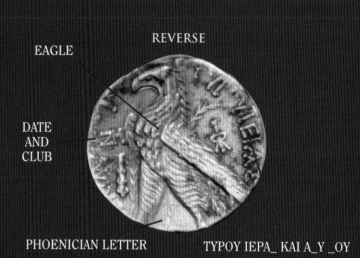

EAGLE

DATE AND CLUB

PHOENICIAN LETTER

TYPOY IEPA_ KAI A_Y _OY

An eagle faces left, standing on the prow of a ship, with a palm over its right wing. The date and club are in the field to the left, and a Phoenician letter is between the eagle's legs. In the right field is the inscription: TYPOY IEPA_ KAI A_Y _OY (of Tyre the holy and inviolable).

OBVERSE

LAUREATE BUST
OF TIBERIUS

TI CAESAR DIVI AVG F AVGVSTVS

REVERSE

REVERSED
SPEAR

LIVIA

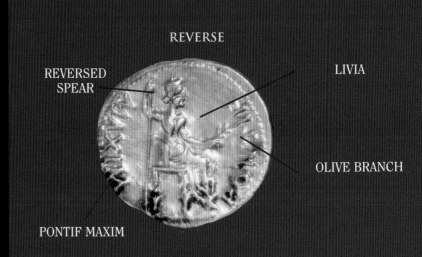

OLIVE BRANCH

PONTIF MAXIM

Laureate bust of Tiberius facing right.
The inscription reads: TI CAESAR DIVI AVG F AVGVSTVS
(Tiberius, Caesar Augustus, Son of the Divine Augustus)

Livia, as Pax, the goddess of peace, seated right on a chair with
ornate legs. She holds an olive branch and a reversed spear.
The inscription reads: PONTIF MAXIM (high priest, another of
the emperor's titles)

THE WIDOW'S MITE

OBVERSE

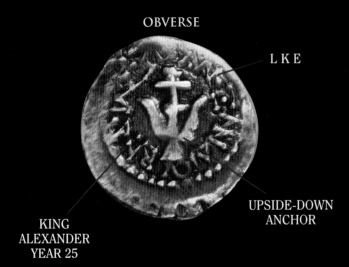

L K E

KING
ALEXANDER
YEAR 25

UPSIDE-DOWN
ANCHOR

Legend reads: King Alexander Year 25. This encircles an upside-down anchor, the symbol of the Seleucid empire's navel strength. Near the anchor points, are the letters L K E which mean year 25.

REVERSE

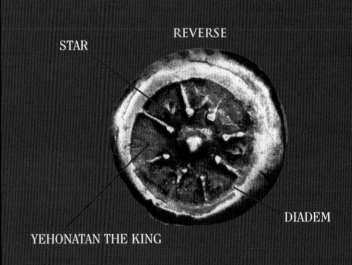

STAR

DIADEM

YEHONATAN THE KING

There is a star with eight rays surrounded by a diadem. This is sometimes also called a spoked wheel.
Between the rays, the legend reads: "Yehonatan the King"

FAMILIAR SYMBOLS ON JEWISH COINS

Anchor: A Seleucid symbol of power, indicating naval strength.

Cornucopia: Hollow animal horn used as a container for many items, also called the "horn of plenty." It was a popular religious symbol, used under the Hasmonean kings and later on coins of Herod the Great and his son. Generally contains fertility symbols such as pomegranates and ears of grain.

Eagle: Universal symbol of power, strength, and pride. It was an emblem of the Roman Empire.

Grapes: Appeared on the coins of the Second Revolt, and grape leaves appeared on the coins of both the First and Second Jewish revolts. Grapes symbolized wine and the grape vine served as a symbol of blessing and fertility. Grapes also represented the blood of Christ.

Lily: Considered first among flowers. Its rapid growth and frailty linked it to fertility. This was used as a symbol in the Jewish Temple. Lilies are also placed on sacred garments and ritual objects.

Owl: Symbolized wisdom and learning. Related to Minerva and Athena, Goddess of Wisdom.

Palm: The palm tree and the palm branch was often featured on Jewish coins. Palms symbolized water, around which they grew. They symbolized fertility and height and were a symbol of Judea because they grew plentifully there.

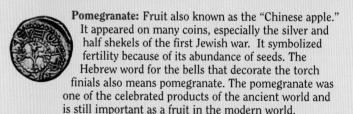

Pomegranate: Fruit also known as the "Chinese apple." It appeared on many coins, especially the silver and half shekels of the first Jewish war. It symbolized fertility because of its abundance of seeds. The Hebrew word for the bells that decorate the torch finials also means pomegranate. The pomegranate was one of the celebrated products of the ancient world and is still important as a fruit in the modern world.

Star: The star's association with the heavens made it a popular symbol. The stars were used to help calculate time, festivals, and important dates. Sometimes the star is encircled by a diadem, the Hellenistic symbol of royalty.

PARABLES CHRIST USED CONCERNING COINS

Christ frequently drew lessons from the common use of coins.

The lost coins is a famous parable:

"I say unto you, that likewise joy shall be in heaven over one sinner that repenteth, more than over ninety and nine just persons, which need no repentance.

Either that woman having ten pieces of silver, if she lose one piece, doth not light a candle, and sweep the house, and seek diligently till she find it?

And when she hath found it she calleth her friends and her neighbors together saying, rejoice with me; for I have found the piece which I had lost.

Likewise I say unto you, there is joy in the presence of the angels of God over one sinner that repenteth" (Luke 15: 7-10).

The parable of the laborers in the vineyard:

"And when he had agreed with the laborers for a penny a day, he sent them into his vineyard.

And when they came they were hired about the eleventh hour, they received every man a penny.

But he answered one of them, and said, Friend, I do thee no wrong: didst not thou agree with me for a penny?" (Matthew 20: 2, 9-10, 13).

The parable question to Simon:

"There was a certain creditor which had two debtors: the one owed five hundred pence, the other fifty: And when they had nothing to pay he frankly forgave them both. Tell me, therefore, which of them will love him most?" (Luke 7: 41).

The parable of the good Samaritan:

"And on the morrow when he departed, he took out two pence and gave them to the host, and said unto him, Take care of him; and whatsoever thou spendest more, when I come again, I will repay thee" (Luke 10: 35).

HOW MUCH WAS MONEY WORTH AT THE TIME?

CONSIDER THESE ESTIMATES FOR WAGES, FOOD, AND LIVESTOCK

- A rabbi made one-half denarius per day

- A vineyard laborer made one denarius per day

- A scribe made two denarii per day

- Bread cost 1/12 of a denarius

- Average size amphora of olive oil cost one denarius

- Cucumber cost one denarius

- An ox cost 100 denarii

- A calf cost 20 denarii

- A lamb cost four denarii

- Two sparrows cost 1/16 denarius

- House rent cost four denarii per month

- Two pigeons cost one denarius

The earliest pieces of metal used as money were hardly coins at all. They were merely rough lumps of precious metal of a specified weight stamped with an authorized seal. Electrum was the first metal used for these early coins. This a is a natural alloy of gold and silver common to Asia Minor, where such coins were produced some seven hundred years before the birth of Christ.

How were these ancient coins made? Finished dies were used to strike blanks of metal. Apparently, these blanks were prepared by casting molten metal in small molds approximately the size of the intended coins. These blanks were then adjusted to the proper weight before going to the coiner.

A heated blank of metal was placed on an anvil that had been engraved to form a rough die. The figure carved into this die was generally a design recognizable as the symbol or authority of the king, or a representation of a local deity. The metal blank was forced into the die by a punch which was hit with a heavy hammer.

The resulting coins bore a raised impression on one side and a ragged impression from the punch on the other side. This early method of minting left much to be desired in the appearance of the coins. They were not necessarily round, often double struck, or made with dies that were cracked or broken, or their designs were not properly centered on the blanks. Nevertheless, they were recognizable, a very accurate measure of precious metal, and acceptable to the people.

Roman coins were minted with more sophisticated implements than those used by earlier cultures. The dies, consisting of carefully engraved obverse and reverse, were fastened to hinged tongs. This arrangement kept the dies in proper alignment when a blank was placed between them and the tongs and then struck with a heavy hammer. These coins were also more uniform in thickness and almost round, though no special care was taken to make them perfectly symmetrical.

DATING ANCIENT COINS

Unlike today's coinage, which is dated in the year it was minted, ancient coins were generally dated by the year of a specific ruler or a specific event, such as a war, or by a local or provincial area. For example, "King Alexander Year 25" might be an inscription and it would mean the coin was made during Alexander's 25th year as a ruler. You must know your history to determine the calendar year in which an ancient coin was manufactured. What a challenge!

Obverse Die

Coin Blank

Anvil

Reverse Die

Punch

JUDEAN TIMELINE

2000-1700 B.C.
Abraham leads his people to Canaan but famine coerces Jacob to lead the Hebrews to Egypt

1300-1260 B.C.
Moses leads the Hebrews out of Egypt

1020 B.C.
Saul becomes the first king of the Hebrews

1000-961 B.C.
King Solomon builds the First Temple

922-722 B.C.
Fighting splits the Kingdom into Israel and Judah.

722 B.C.
Assyrians conquer northern kingdom of Israel and Jews are killed or deported. They are known as the "ten lost tribes."

142 B.C.
Jews under Maccabaeus revolt and regain control of Judah.

167 B. C.
Antiochus IV outlawed Judaism and ordered everyone to worship Greek gods.

198 B.C.
Antiochus IV of Syria conquers Judah

332 B.C.
Alexander the Great defeats the Persians and conquers their territory.

539 B.C.
Persians defeat Babylonians and allow Jews to return to Judah and rebuild their temple

586 B.C.
Babylonians capture Judah, destroy the temple and move Jews to Babylon and enslave them.

63 B.C.
Civil war weakens Judah; Roman general Pompey takes over the country and Judah becomes a Roman province renamed Judea.

37 B.C.
Herod the Great rules Judea until his death in 4 A.D.

29 A.D
Jesus crucified

66 A.D.
Jews revolt against Rome but are destroyed along with the temple

132 A.D.
Jews, led by Simon Bar-Kochba, rebel again but are destroyed.

135 A.D
The diaspora begins.

COIN COLLECTING

People collect for many reasons: fun, knowledge, and investment. Whatever the motivation, please consider the following criteria when purchasing ancient coinage:

Aesthetic or "eye appeal" (what keeps drawing you to a coin)

Demand (what the current market value of a coin is)

Denomination (larger coins are generally more expensive than smaller ones)

Detail (whether they are well-centered and well-struck)

Fame (the fame or notoriety—as in Nero's case—of the person issuing the coin)

Historical Value (the reason a coin was issued helps determine its value)

Metal (gold is generally the most expensive metal)

Pedigree (who previously owned the coins)

Rarity (how many coins of a type are available)

Surface (whether there is wear, an abrasion, or a gouge)

GRADING ANCIENT COINS

In addition to these criteria for coin collecting, one should also consider a coin's grade, but with the knowledge that all grading is subjective. With that caveat in mind, consider that ancient coins generally fall into four grade categories:

Good: Very worn

Fine: Still has some detail in the motif and most legends will be readable

Very Fine: Moderate wear. Legends are fully readable and the subject clearly recognizable

Extra Fine: Little wear. All legends sharp and clear

However, these categories are often qualified with terms such as choice or the finest known specimen. Remember: the grade is important but only in relation to other considerations. You are the buyer. You set the priorities.

HISTORICAL MAPS

Israel and Judah

722 B.C. Assyrians invade northern kingdom of Israel and inhabitants flee. 586 B.C. Babylonians invade southern kingdom of Judah.

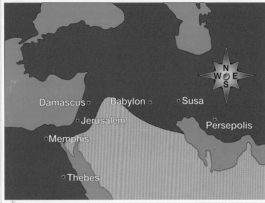

Persian Empire

539 B.C. Cyrus, King of Persia allows Jewish people to return to Israel.
332 B.C. Persian empire falls to Alexander the Great.

Roman Province

63 B.C. Romans invade and occupy Jerusalem.